A Visit to the Doctor

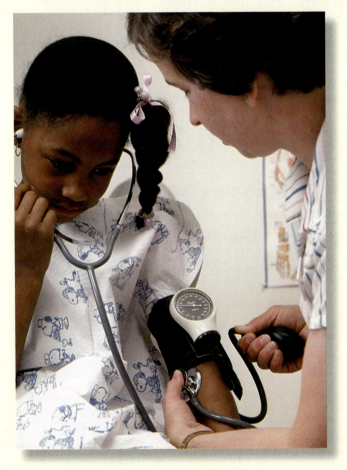

By Marcie Aboff

CELEBRATION PRESS
Pearson Learning Group

Contents

Going to the Doctor 3

Measuring Temperature 4

Measuring Height and Weight 5

Growth Charts 8

Listening to Heart Rate 10

Measuring Blood Pressure 11

Other Tools Doctors Use 13

Glossary 15

Index 16

Going to the Doctor

Many people go to a doctor when they are sick. Many people also visit the doctor when they are well. These people go for a **checkup**. Whether you are sick or healthy, a doctor or nurse uses math when checking your health.

A doctor or nurse uses numbers to record information about your health.

Measuring Temperature

During a checkup, a nurse uses a **thermometer** to measure a patient's temperature. Temperature is measured in degrees **Fahrenheit** (°F).

Normal body temperature is between 97°F and 100°F. A patient with a temperature above 100°F could have a fever.

Changing Body Temperature

Body temperature can change. At night, before going to bed, body temperature is slightly lower. During the day, while the body moves around, body temperature is slightly higher.

A thermometer measures body temperature.

Measuring Weight and Height

Doctors and nurses use numbers to measure **weight** and **height**. They use scales to measure weight. They use tape measures or height rods to measure height.

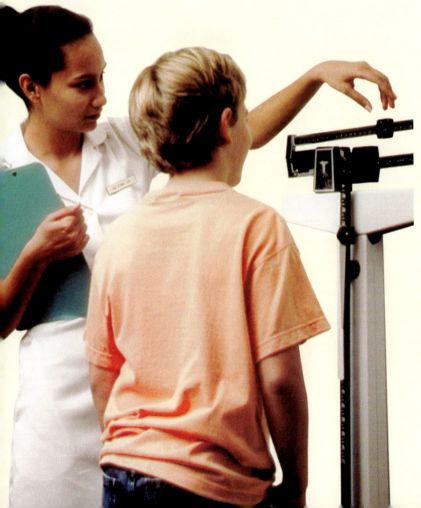

Numbers on a scale show the patient's weight.

A special scale is used to measure a baby's weight. A baby sits or lies on the scale. The scale shows how many **pounds** and **ounces** the baby weighs.

A doctor uses a tape measure to see how long a baby is. A baby's height is measured in inches.

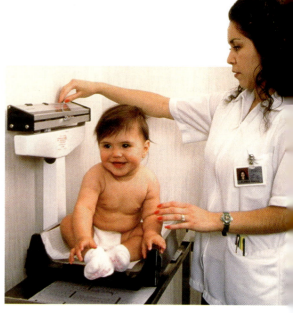

measuring a baby's weight

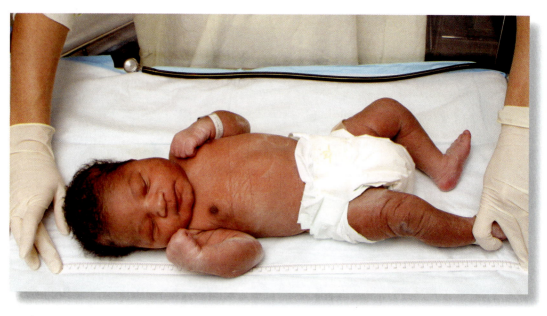

measuring a baby's height

To measure the weight of older patients, the patient stands on a scale. The scale has a metal bar with weights that point to numbers. The numbers tell the patient's weight in pounds.

Some scales also have a height rod to measure the patient's height. The rod measures height in inches.

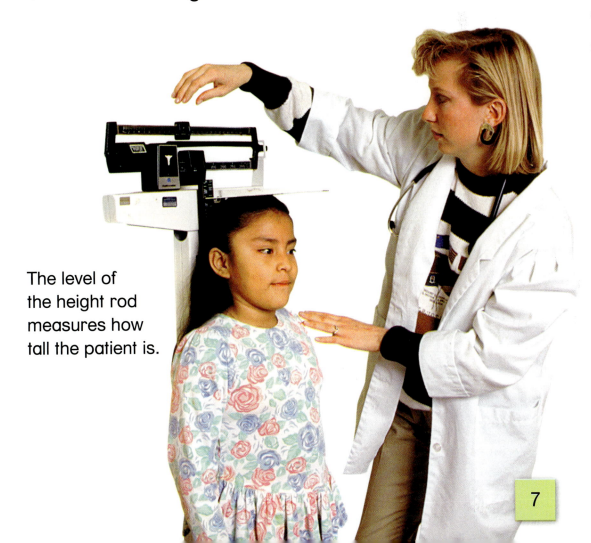

The level of the height rod measures how tall the patient is.

Growth Charts

A doctor uses measurement to **compare** a patient's growth to the growth of other children who are the same age. A doctor uses a **growth chart**.

A growth chart is actually a **graph**. There are lines on the graph. The areas above and below the lines show how children in the same age group can have different height or weight.

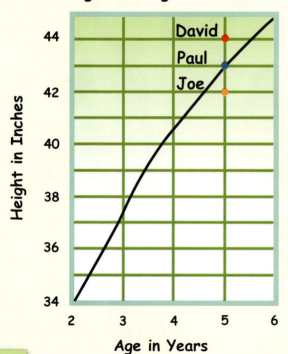

This is a line from a growth chart. The heights of three five-year-old boys are marked on the chart. David is taller than half the boys his age. Paul is as tall as half the boys his age. Joe is shorter than half the boys his age.

When using a growth chart, a doctor first measures the patient's height or weight. The doctor then marks the measurement on the growth chart.

The doctor can tell how the patient's height compares to the height of other children the same age. The doctor can also compare the patient's weight to the weight of other children the same age.

These children are all the same age but have different heights.

Listening to Heart Rate

A doctor also uses math when he or she listens to a patient's heart. During a checkup, the doctor places a stethoscope against the patient's chest. He or she carefully listens to the heartbeats. A doctor may count the number of heartbeats to make sure a patient's heart is healthy.

A doctor uses a stethoscope to listen to a patient's heart rate.

Heart Rate

The normal heart rate for a baby that is resting is between 100 and 160 beats a minute. The normal resting heart rate for a patient between the ages of 1 and 10 years is between 70 and 120 beats a minute.

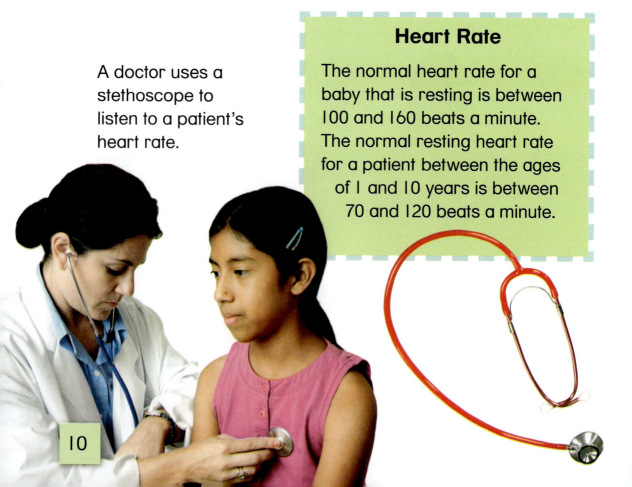

Measuring Blood Pressure

A nurse records numbers when measuring a patient's blood pressure. Blood pressure is the force of blood moving through blood vessels. Different instruments are used to measure how well blood flows in a patient's body.

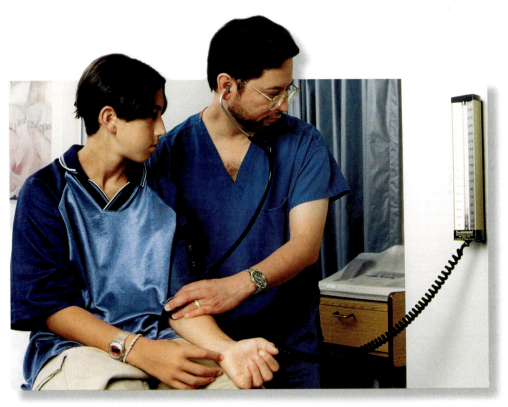

measuring blood pressure

A nurse uses a stethoscope to listen to the blood flowing in the patient's arm. As a cuff gently squeezes the patient's arm, the nurse also watches liquid rise inside a special instrument. Blood pressure is measured by reading the level of the liquid two times.

The nurse records the two numbers. The numbers tell if the patient has normal, high, or low blood pressure. High or low blood pressure may indicate an illness.

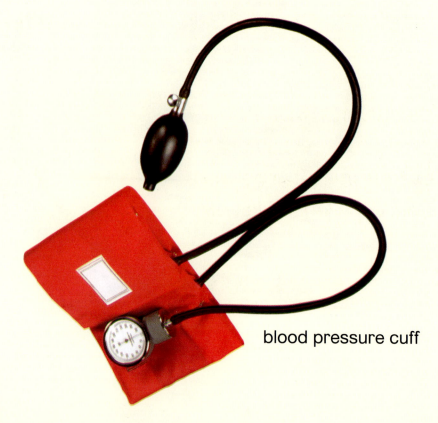

blood pressure cuff

Other Tools Doctors Use

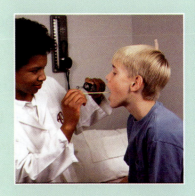

A doctor does not need math to examine every part of a patient. A doctor uses a tongue depressor to look into a patient's mouth. The doctor also uses special tools that have a light. These tools help the doctor examine a patient's eyes, ears, and mouth.

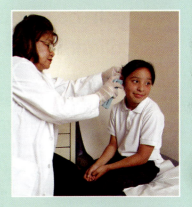

The doctor may also test a patient's nerves. He or she gently taps below a patient's knee with a **reflex hammer**. It is normal for the patient's leg to kick out.

Some tools do not require a doctor to use math when examining a patient.

During checkups, doctors and nurses use a lot of math. Charts, scales, and measuring rods are used to check a patient's growth. Numbers are used to record information, such as temperature and blood pressure. A doctor or nurse may count a patient's heartbeats. Math helps doctors and nurses to know if their patients are healthy.

A doctor uses numbers to record information about a patient on a chart.

Glossary

checkup a visit to a doctor to see if a person is healthy

compare to look at two or more things to see how they are alike or different

Fahrenheit (°F) a unit of temperature

graph a chart that shows the relationship between two or more changing things

growth chart a graph that shows the height or weight of children in a certain age group

height measurement from head to foot

ounces standard units used to measure weight; there are 16 ounces in a pound

pounds standard units used to measure weight

reflex hammer a soft hammer used to test nerves in the body

thermometer a tool used to measure temperature

weight how heavy something is

Index

blood pressure 11–12, 14

checkup 3, 4, 10, 14

Fahrenheit 4

growth chart 8–9

height 5, 6, 7, 8, 9

inches 6, 7

ounces 6

pounds 6–7

reflex hammer 13

scale 5–7, 14

stethoscope 10, 12

temperature 4, 14

thermometer 4

tongue depressor 13

weight 5, 6, 7, 8, 9